MEDIEVAL LIVES

Peasant

ROBERT HULL

FRANKLIN WATTS
LONDON•SYDNEY

First published in 2008 by Franklin Watts

Franklin Watts
338 Euston Road
London NW1 3BH

Franklin Watts Australia
Level 17/207 Kent Street
Sydney, NSW 2000

A CIP catalogue record for this book is available
from the British Library.

Dewey number: 940.1

ISBN 978 0 7496 7737 4

Printed in China

Franklin Watts is a division of Hachette Children's
Books, an Hachette Livre UK company.

Artwork: Gillian Clements
Editor: Sarah Ridley
Editor in chief: John C. Miles
Designer: Simon Borrough
Art director: Jonathan Hair
Picture research: Diana Morris

Picture credits:
Arquivo Nacional da Torre do Tombo Lisbon/Alfredo Dali Orti/The Art Archive: 21. British Library, London, Courtesy of the Board of Trustees: 26. British Library, London/The Art Archive: front cover, 11t, 20, 24, 29t, 33t, 33b, 36. British Library, London/Bridgeman Art Library: 14, 41. British Library, London/HIP/Topfoto: 27. Biblioteca Nazionale Marciana, Venice/Gianni Dagli Orti/The Art Archive: 35. Bibliothèque Nationale, Paris/AKG Images : 24. Bibliothèque Nationale, Paris/Bridgeman Art Library: 23t. Bodleian Library, Oxford/The Art Archive : 23b, 30. Chris Howes/Wild Places/Alamy: 13. Lambeth Palace Library, London: Bridgeman Art Library: 10. Musée des Beaux Arts, Ghent/Topfoto: 19t. Musée Condé, Chantilly/Giraudon/Bridgeman Art Library: 16, 18, 38, 40. Museo Civico Bologna/Gianni Dagli Orti/The Art Archive: 34. Museo Civico Città di Castello/Gianni Dagli Orti/The Art Archive: 39. The Museum of London: 15t. Picturepoint/Topham: 5, 8. Private Collection, Switzerland/AKG Images: 37t. Roy Rainford/Robert Harding Picture Library: 17. Ann Ronan PL/HIP/Topfoto: 31. Victoria and Albert Museum, London/Graham Brandon/The Art Archive: 28.

Every attempt has been made to clear copyright. Should there be any inadvertent omission please apply to the publisher for rectification.

CONTENTS

INTRODUCTION

The medieval period of European history runs from about 1000 to about 1500. It was a time of momentous events. In 1066 England was conquered by the Norman French king, William the Conqueror, and his nobles. During most of the 14th century, France and England fought a series of wars called the Hundred Years War. In addition, Christian crusaders fought with Muslim Arab armies over the control of Jerusalem. And the disease known as the Black Death struck in 1348, killing around one third of the population of Europe.

A peasant sows seeds. The medieval economy was based on agriculture.

Feudal society

At the beginning of this period, European society was thoroughly 'feudal'. Kings owned all the land, but barons were granted land in return for service in war. Nobles made similar arrangements with knights, and they in turn with those below them, down to the peasants, who were granted a few acres of land, in return for fees and work obligations. This network of agreements held society together.

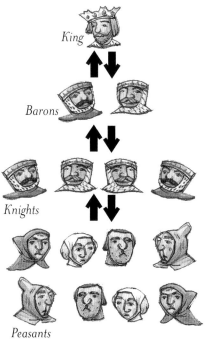

King

Barons

Knights

Peasants

Throughout the medieval period, great building projects went on – of monasteries and abbeys, castles, churches and cathedrals. Towns and trade flourished and grew yet farming remained as important as ever. Most people worked on land that they did not own. In return, farmers owed work and fees (money, animals or goods) to the lord or lady of the manor.

The peasant farmer

In many parts of Europe, the peasant farmer worked alongside others on strips of land scattered across two or three huge fields surrounding a village. In some areas fields were arranged differently, and farmhouses stood on their own, or in small hamlets. The peasant was 'tied' to this land. He had to stay in one place if he wanted to carry on cultivating his few acres. If he ran away, as some peasants did, he would have no land to farm. He would be punished too, if he were caught.

In many ways, his life was not his own; he was a 'serf', halfway between free man and outright owned slave. Unlike a slave, he had important rights that were also part of the custom of the village, like the right to take timber for houses from woodland, or the right to speak in the village assembly, the 'hall-moote'.

The 'peasant'

The peasant whose life we follow in this book is typical of those peasants who worked about 20 to 30 acres of land, and lived in a village of perhaps 50 houses. We say 'peasant' but that word did not come into English until the 15th century. Our peasant was 'servile', a serf or 'husbondman' (a man bound to the land), with a house.

The peasant was seldom well-off, and often miserably poor. He ate well when harvests were good but famine struck often. Any of his children might die young, or his wife in childbirth. In times of need he relied on his neighbours. Otherwise the peasant lived his life in a long struggle with the land, the demands of his lord, violence and the ever-present risk of disease, illness and death. Yet he often managed to enjoy life – he made the best of it.

Piers the Plowman

This is part of a poem about Piers the Plowman (ploughman) written by the 14th century English poet, William Langland:

❖ *His hood was full of holes and his hair stuck out of it. As he walked his toes peered out from his worn shoes... He was all be-daubed with mud as he followed the plough. He had two thin mittens with worn-out fingers that were thick with muck. This man was almost up to his ankles in mud as he drove along four heifers [young cows] that were so feeble, such a sorry-looking sight, you could count every rib they had.* ❖

Serf or slave?

Nothing was the serf's own. Even his children counted as the lord's possessions, as is shown by this 11th century French document that shares out serfs and their children:

❖ *We, the monks of Marmoutier and Gautier Renaud, held in common men and women serfs, who were to be divided between us...Therefore, in the year of Our Lord 1087... in the time of Abbot Bernard, we proceeded to the division of the male and female children of several families.* ❖

Those names are then listed, and the document closes with:

❖ *There was excepted from the division one very young girl-child, who remained in her cradle. If she lives, she is to be our common property until an agreement is made to assign her to one or the other lordship.* ❖

9

FIRST YEARS

The peasant baby is born at home, in the parents' bed. At the birth, the mother is helped by female neighbours and a midwife. Any birth, whatever class you belong to, is very risky. For every child who survives there are usually little sisters and brothers who don't. If things go wrong in childbirth, as they sometimes do, there is little that can be done. The mother dies, or the child, or both. But this mother is well and a baby boy arrives safely.

In medieval times, as many as one in four babies died in their first year; another one in eight before their fourth birthday, and a further one in 15 before the age of nine. So nearly 40 per cent of all children born died before their 10th birthday.

Baby days

The baby is washed carefully and wrapped in swaddling clothes, long strips of cloth bound around the body. They are constricting but are supposed to help limbs grow straight.

After a few days, when she is strong enough, his mother is 'churched' at a service of purification in the village church, and the baby is 'baptised' at the font. He is now a member of the Catholic Church. He is given a first name, that of one of the three godparents nominated to help with his upbringing. If he had died unbaptised he would have gone to Hell, according to the Church.

The baby feeds on breast-milk until he is about 18 months. His first solid food is chewed for him in his mother's mouth, and given to him on her finger.

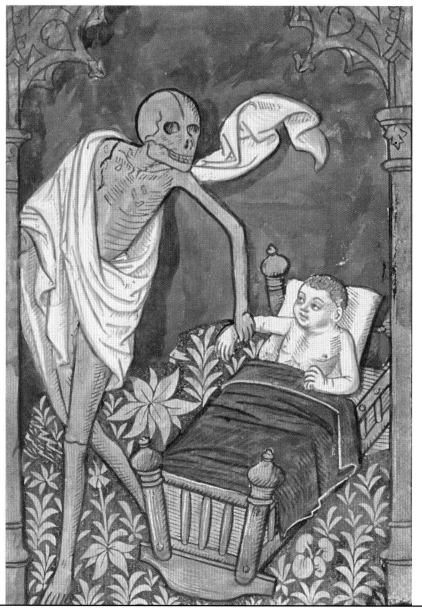

Death comes for a child in this manuscript illustration.

Toddling

Soon he is toddling about, and needs to be watched every minute. When he starts to walk he has a kind of walking frame to help him – and prevent a fall or a hurried dash leading to one. He might go too near the hearth-fire, or the cooking-pot. There are animals everywhere. A wandering pig out of its pen has a nasty bite. He easily gets dirty roaming about the house and outside in the lanes.

As he grows older, the little boy joins his older brothers and sisters in a shared bed. He is sung to, and told stories and little rhymes.

There is much watching to do in the first years. Inside the house he watches his mother cooking over the hearth, brewing ale, spinning wool. He watches his father carving wooden bowls, shaping stakes or weaving basket fish traps.

Outside is just as interesting. There are pigs rootling in the fenced yard, birds taking seeds, callers coming down the lane, ploughs and carts rolling by.

A peasant woman holds a baby indoors while a man chops wood outside in the snow.

PEASANT COTTAGE

The young peasant's home is a small house in a village. It consists of three bays or rooms: a bedroom, a 'hall' or living area with a stone hearth, and a stall. It's smoky at times, and can be cold and damp.

The house has a frame of curved timbers. They were cut from a suitable tree some distance away, and brought to the village by the specialist carpenters who did much of the work. They mounted the frame on stones, so the wood is above damp ground to prevent rot.

The church and village green with its pond were at the heart of most medieval villages.

Medieval facts

Peasant houses across Europe varied in building style and design, in size, in the number of rooms and areas — including animal stalls and floors for threshing, as well as bedrooms and living areas — and in the arrangement of space. Building materials varied less. In northern countries wood was used, but stone was easier to come by near the Mediterranean, in Italy and southern France. In later medieval times stone was increasingly used for wealthier peasant houses.

Roof and rooms

Materials for the roof and walls are easy to find. The roof is thatched with reeds and straw, and the walls are made from strips of thin wood (wattles) filled in with clay and animal dung (daub).

The house is about 12 metres long – longer than some in the village, not so long as others – and is about 5 metres wide. It probably cost about £6 to build.

At one end of the hall space, on the earth floor, is an open hearth with a fire for cooking. There is no chimney so smoke from the fire drifts out of the door or through the window-openings, which have shutters and are covered with cloth in cold weather. Straw covers the floor.

Furnishings

The family has a few pieces of furniture: a locked chest for best clothes, frames for the straw-filled mattresses, a table, a bench, stools, a tub for washing, a broom. They have mugs and plates of pottery and wood and even a jug of coarse glass, bought from town craftsmen, and spoons of horn, as well as various other craft-made articles.

The house is detached, fenced in its own 'messuage' or space, with a byre for animals, and an outhouse to keep various implements in, like the cart, which neighbours sometimes borrow, and don't bring back until asked! There is about half an acre of garden at the back to grow vegetables, herbs and fruit. At the front is a dung-hill which will be used as fertiliser. The whole plot is surrounded by hedges and a wall, so there's some feeling of privacy, and the door of the house has a lock.

From about the 13th century onwards, farmhouses might be constructed of stone in areas where stone was plentiful. This photo shows a modern reconstruction.

Smoke-free zone

In later medieval Germany the invention of the heated stove – the stube – meant that bigger peasant houses could be kept more or less smoke-free. The heated living room is a theme in poems by Neidhart von Reuental:

❖ *Megenwart's stube is large enough. Let's have a dance there on Sunday! His daughter says spread the news and come. Engelmar's preparing for dancing round the table.*❖

CHILDHOOD

From about the age of three onwards the little peasant boy plays, and plays. He plays with stones he picks up; he throws sticks in the stream and makes dams there. He and his young friends make pretend houses and boats; they have little bows and arrows. They play cherry-pit, rolling cherry stones to drop into holes, and marbles.

They have their slangy talk and rhymes, too, and their cheeky calling games. They have little carved animals and carts, some homemade, one or two bought from craftsmen at the market, or from travelling pedlars, 'chapmen'.

Play and games

The little boy mostly plays with other children, out in the lane or street or in the fields, often alongside his father as he works. The village has its dangers – mill-ponds and streams, horses with iron-shod hooves, cattle with long horns, pigs with fierce bites, even wolves sometimes; but he and his friends are free to roam and rove, though not too far.

Spoilt children

A 13th century French sermon given by a priest suggests that peasant children were spoilt at first, then treated more harshly:
❖ *Peasants spoil their children and make them little red frocks, and then, when they are a little bit older, they put them to the plough.* ❖

Medieval boys enjoy a swim.

This carved toy knight would have been a child's prize possession.

When they are older, they play running and throwing and balancing games. 'Buck hide' is a kind of hide-and-seek; the 'buck' hides from the hunter. Some games are seasonal. Climbing for nuts and fruit in autumn is fun – a game, not work.

In Lent the child spins a top, as all the boys do. In early winter, after the pigs are killed, pigs' bladders become balloons, 'with many beans or peasen put within', or are inflated and wrapped with cloth to make footballs.

Education for all

In all ranks of society there were parents who wanted their children educated. In the monk Aelfric's Colloquy, a teaching aid written in 1005, the teacher asks:

❖ *Who are you here before me? Us boys.* ❖

The boys are the sons of ploughmen, shepherds, fishermen, merchants, shoemakers, bakers and so on.

Growing up

The peasant boy is growing up fast but he is not at school. Sometimes his father sends him to the parish priest to learn to spell out and read letters, and to sing too. His friend's father decides his son should go off to the neighbouring monastery, to be educated and study Latin to become a monk.

The young peasant prepares for his father's world of work, too. He drives ducks to the pond, collects hens' eggs, fetches water from the well. He goes with his father to the fields and has a stick to help drive the oxen along in front of the plough. He has to be careful; helping with cattle and horses can lead to accidents. Then, when he is 12, his father arranges for him to work a few days each week on the church's home farm, and earn a penny or two.

Medieval facts

By the time they were around the age of 14, children had their place in the world decided by law. The Church believed that, until they were 14, children were too young to commit sinful acts. The laws said children could not marry until then, or take communion, and did not have to make confession to the priest.

THE CHURCH

The parish church is at the centre of the village, and village life. From baptism to wedding to funeral, the most solemn moments of everyone's lives are celebrated or commemorated there.

Despite the church's importance, and the role of the priest in the parish, he is only just literate. He only knows the Mass by heart, not the meaning of its Latin words. He is not well-off, either. He has to work the church's own land, the 'glebe', and has been known to store corn and keep sheep in the church.

The farmer-priest

The priest was often a part-time farmer. Sometimes farming and religion clashed. In 1302 the parishioners of St Mary's Church in Devon complained that their vicar:

❖ ...keeps all manner of his beasts in the churchyard, by which it is badly trampled and vilely fouled...The same vicar also has his malt prepared in the church and keeps his corn and other things therein...❖

Peasants work hard to help support the priest in this manuscript picture.

Gathering tithes

A 14th century handbook for priests written by John de Burgo has this suggestion to help priests gather tithes:

❖ Let peasants be questioned in the confessional whether they have defrauded by withholding or diminishing their tithes;... whether they have withheld their bounden service to their lords.❖

Church upkeep

Much of the priest's living comes from crops and cattle and sometimes money that the village peasants pay in 'tithes' – tenths. In this way the young peasant's father helps pay for the upkeep of the church. In theory, he gives the priest a tenth of all he produces, and earns, every year. Cattle and crops are called 'great tithes'; others, hens and eggs and so on, 'lesser tithes'. When the peasant dies, the church can take from his family a kind of death tax – a 'mortuary' – which is usually the second-best animal; the lord has the best.

On Sunday the family's best clothes come out of the wooden chest for Mass. The colourful wall paintings in the church depict God, the Virgin Mary and Jesus, heaven and hell, birth and marriage, sin, good and evil, love, hate and good conduct. The young peasant cannot read but finds them very solemn.

In the church

Everyone in the family goes to church. The young and the very young talk and even scamper about while the adults pay attention. The priest conducts the service in the chancel where the altar is, behind the wooden screen. The congregation prays or repeats his words on the other side of the screen, in the nave.

The church bells ring not just for Mass and other religious festivals, but to warn villagers of emergencies, and to summon them to hear news. It is truly the villagers' church, used as a refuge sometimes, or a courthouse, to brew ale or store corn in, even as a prison.

The churchyard

And the churchyard is used for anything from burials to games and festivities, singing and dancing, something the Church often says it objects to. There is a story that some peasants found dancing in the churchyard on Christmas Eve were changed into trees for a year – 'rooted to the spot'.

Tithe barns, such as this English example, stored the portion of the harvest owed to the Church.

Reading in church

An Italian visitor to England in 1500 noted an interesting English habit – taking books to church:

❖ *They all attend Mass every day, those who can read taking the office of Our Lady with them, and with some companion reading it in the church, verse by verse, in the manner of churchmen.* ❖

MARRIAGE ·

By the time the young peasant is 20, he wants to marry. To do so he needs his father's consent. That will only be given when his father is ready to hand over the tenement holding to the son, and the son's wife, or when the son can provide his parents with a cottage and garden. Either that, or the father needs to be sure that he and his wife can carry on living in the family house, too.

A priest reads the marriage service for the wedding of a young couple in this manuscript illustration.

Negotiating a marriage

The next step is for the father to look around for a partner for his son. He will consider the daughters of men of his own status. Once a prospective bride is found, a go-between will be sent to her family to talk about a possible marriage. If everyone agrees, the young people will spend some time together for the next month or two, to see how they get on.

If all these stages go well, the young woman's father will bring her over to view her prospective husband's house and holding. The fathers will thrash out the business side of the union, especially what dowry the young woman will bring from her family and what land the young peasant will have. The girl's father will also pay a fine to his lord to receive permission for his daughter to marry.

Brueghel's painting from the 1400s shows people serving food at a wedding banquet.

The 'wed'

On the wedding day, there are two ceremonies, one at the church door and one inside the church. Outside the church the young peasant names the gift dower he is giving his bride, and places gold or silver, and a ring for her, on a shield or book, with some pennies for the poor. They exchange vows, the priest sprinkles the ring with holy water and blesses it, and passes it to the peasant to place on his bride's middle finger. 'With this ring I thee wed,' he says, then gives her the gold and says, 'And with this gold I thee honour.'

They enter the church and there the priest celebrates a Nuptial (wedding) Mass. Towards the end of the service, he covers the couple symbolically with a 'care-cloth'.

Afterwards, there is merry-making and dancing in the churchyard, and games, and a 'bride-ale' begins, leading to the supper which the bride's father agreed to provide.

'Troth-plight'

In the eyes of the Church, the young peasant and his possible bride have to consent to what is happening. If they agree, and make promises to each other, even in private, that private 'troth-plight' is, for the Church, a binding contract which its courts will enforce as a marriage.

There needs to be a public agreement to marry – the 'betrothal', with a public 'troth-plight' or 'hand-fasting'. The priest calls the banns at church, informing villagers of the forthcoming marriage, and asking anyone who believes there is any reason for them not to marry to speak up.

Husbands rule

A 12th century Welsh law says that wives need the husband's permission to dispose of things or even lend them, and even then only to neighbours within shouting distance:

❖ *The wife of a villein may not give away anything without her husband's permission except her head-dress; and she cannot lend anything except her sieve and griddle, and that only as far as her cry may be heard when her foot is on her threshold.* ❖

Medieval facts

A baby might be born to a couple before the wedding. The baby was made 'legitimate' in the eyes of the Church and the world by being placed under the care-cloth during the last part of the Nuptial Mass.

LAND

Teamwork

In the open fields of Wales, peasants worked together on each other's strips of land:

❖ *Whoever intends to engage on co-tillage with others, it is right for them all to undertake to do so, by mutually joining hands.* ❖

The young peasant's father has agreed to pass his house and land – his tenement – to his son. The newly-married peasant and his wife share the house with his father and mother. The house is part of a 'messuage'; it has a piece of land, or 'croft', attached to it. The new wife, helped by her mother-in-law, will grow vegetables there, and look after the fruit trees and the pigs and hens. She may decide to grow flax and hemp for rope and dye stuffs. It is an important part of the family's farming.

Medieval facts

The way the land was ploughed, from the strip's centre outwards, turning the sod inwards to the right, tended to heap the earth up in ridges, with furrows developing between, which helped drainage. The vestiges of this pattern of ridge and furrow still survive in some places.

Commons and open fields

At the edge of the village is 'common' grazing land, grazing that anyone's cattle can be pastured on, in restricted numbers to prevent over-grazing. That is where the peasant and his wife keep most of their cattle, for milk, butter and cheese, and their sheep, for wool. The village cattle-herd and shepherd are there to look after the animals.

Most of the peasant's back-breaking labour takes place in the large, 'open' fields. An open field is one in which every farmer in the village has his own strips of land to work. Widths and shapes vary but tend to be narrow. Many are a furlong – a 'furrow long' – in length. Some are longer, even reaching from the village to its boundary.

The strip arrangement is fair to everyone. Every farmer has a share of the best and the worst land, and shares equally in the chances of good or bad harvests.

Ploughing with oxen, from an English manuscript, the Luttrell Psalter. *A psalter was a prayer book.*

Crop rotation

The three village fields are 'rotated'. A field may be sown with wheat one year, with beans the next year; the third year it will lie 'fallow', uncultivated, though cattle will graze there, and manure will help it recover its fertility.

The peasant needs oxen for ploughing, and a helper. He will borrow oxen sometimes and rely on other peasants for their labour and the loan of a plough. Most ploughs in the village are owned by wealthy peasants, or by groups of peasants. The peasant will need most of the grain he harvests from his 20 scattered acres to feed his family and to keep as seed for next year. But he will hope to sell some of it, perhaps a third or a quarter.

He will also hope to make money from carting wood for fuel, as well as the wood he can take for fencing. The larger trees on his land will be useful for timber. His wife keeps a few hives under the trees for gathering honey.

Medieval facts

Not all peasants had rights of inheritance. In 1305 Scottish peasants petitioned Edward I (when he was occupying Scotland) for the same rights of inheritance as peasants in England.

Young people dance to bagpipe music while sheep graze.

WORK-SERVICE FOR THE MANOR

The peasant does not own the land he now works. He is a tenant, and not a free tenant, but a villein. He inherits his villein status, with the land, from his father. That means he owes his lord days of work throughout his lifetime.

By hook or by crook — fallen branches helped to keep peasants warm.

Work-days and 'boon-days'

The work-days, fees and rents the peasant owes the lord are fixed by custom and recorded on the manor's court roll. It is three days a week, throughout the year. The lord can also demand extra days of work – 'boon-days' or 'love-days' – in emergencies, which of course are the lord's emergencies. If it rains on some of the days when the peasants should be cutting hay for the lord, the lord may demand a 'boon' of extra days' work from his tenants. They will lose time spent on their own haymaking. At least on boon-days the lord has to provide food and ale.

Medieval facts

The peasant had rights according to custom. They often had the right to pick up fallen wood for fires, or to take any dead or dangling branches they could knock from trees. Hence the expression, 'by hook or by crook'.

In this manuscript painting for the capital letter 'E', peasants pay the tax collector.

The fines and services owed to the lord vary greatly. This means that the reeve, the official appointed from amongst the peasants to look after the lord's interests and see the fines and dues are paid, is very busy and not popular.

The peasant also pays collective village taxes, taxes every villein pays. For instance, a 'recognition' fine is demanded when a new lord inherits his estate. 'Tallage' is a tax for little else than occupying the land. His poorer neighbours often pay their dues in pots and pans, beehives, or whatever they can.

Not surprisingly, because work on the lord's land means losing time and work on his own land, the peasant works less hard and efficiently for the lord than he does for himself. Some lords find it cheaper to hire workers, especially as to feed the peasants on boon-days can outstrip profits. Lords are sometimes willing to exchange the peasant's work-days for a cash payment from them; that suits some peasants.

Fees and fines

Just as much resented as the work-days are the fees or fines the lord takes on certain occasions. The peasant paid a fine to take over his father's land. When he dies his wife will pay 'heriot', a death duty of the 'best beast'. For every 'right' the peasant or his wife has, there seems to be a corresponding fine, expressed as 'pork-due', 'chicken-fine', or whatever it is.

Servants bake loaves in a bread oven.

THE MANORIAL COURT

The young peasant has been to the lord's court with his father at various times since he was 12. Now he has to 'pay suit' there whenever it meets, which varies from once every three weeks to three times a year. Someone acting for him will need to present the court with a good reason for his absence if he's not there, or he'll pay a fine.

Court records

The court regulates and records details of the life of the village: its disputes, details of labour services, the fines and dues that peasants owe, and failures to pay them. Offences like trespass and theft and violence of a minor kind, such as attacks on manor officials, brawls and fights, are all dealt with in the court.

The peasant is told in advance when the court will meet. The lord of the manor, or one of his top officials – the cellarer or the steward – makes the judgements. Other officials are present: hayward, ale-tasters, 'tithing-men', reeve and bailiff.

All the peasant's agreements and transactions, and of course his father's before him, anything to do with land, property, work, wages and his legal status are recorded there, on the court rolls; all fines, and fees and details of inheritance. If the peasant wishes to know what the 'custom' of the manor is for him, he can find out from the roll, with the help of someone who can read, usually the clerk of the court himself.

Although it doesn't depict peasants, this picture shows men paying dues to their overlord.

A medieval court – in this case a royal court – with an offender being hanged (on the right).

The court's work

The peasant is familiar with the work of the court. In court his father hands over the family tenancy to him legally. First he relinquishes the land, and it reverts to the lord. Then the young peasant has to ask permission to take on his father's land himself. According to custom, tenancies are inherited but the lord's right to it has to be acknowledged. The peasant pays his entry fine to the court, in effect to the lord, and the tenancy is his.

One man wants his daughter to work outside the village. Another asks permission to send his son to school in the town. The lord is in theory losing the possible future services of a tenant so a fine is due. One peasant has put too many animals on the common grazing land. Another, who's allowed his house to get delapidated, has had a stake driven in the ground in front of it, to say the lord wants it repaired. Others have failed to report for haymaking on the lord's land, and have spoken impudently to the hayward.

Much of it is routine, but occasionally dramatic stories appear; the death by drowning of a small child, the killing of a peasant. In all cases involving deaths, accidental or not, a Royal coroner has to be present.

Medieval facts

The right to erect a gallows and hang people belonged to the monarch but some lords, nonetheless, did so themselves. The Abbot of Crowland was convicted of hanging a man who stole 16 eggs – though not on the Abbot's land. The Abbot claimed the right not only of 'ingangenethef', the right to hang a thief caught on his own land, but of 'outfangenethef', the right to hang a man he caught beyond the bounds of his manor.

Mid-winter, especially the Christmas period, is a fine time of year for the peasant. He can take it easy for a few days and sometimes sit by the fire drinking, or play with his children. One year's work is done, the next not yet begun. There will always be hens to feed and fences to mend, but the back-breaking seasonal work has not started.

Endless work

Once this brief respite is over, the year is a round of non-stop working activities decided on by routine and custom. The only interruptions to it are the lord's unpredictable boon-work demands (see pages 22-23), the equally unpredictable weather, feasts and festivals and, of course, illness.

The peasant has to sow, plough and harrow his and his co-worker's strips in the open field, and harvest the hay, wheat, barley, oats, rye, peas and beans. He has to look after the pigs and shear the sheep.

This page from a medieval calendar shows peasants in a winter scene.

Singing ploughmen

A 13th-century book tells ploughmen to be cheerful:

❖ *Ploughmen ought not to be gloomy or irritable, but sing and be cheerful, and encourage the oxen in front of them with their songs. They need to take the cattle their straw and their feed, and to be fond of them, and stay with them in the stable at night. They need to make a fuss of them... When the ploughing is finished it is the duty of the ploughman and the husbandman to look after ditches, to dig, and fence, and repair all the watercourses in the fields, and do various other small useful jobs.* ❖

Spring and summer

By February the peasant's hard year is underway. In March there is the pruning to do. In April there is sowing, ploughing and harrowing. As soon as things start growing there is weeding, and birds to scare off. In June the hay will need cutting. By Lammas (1st August) the cattle have to be let out onto the meadows to feed there until spring.

July is the beginning of harvest, the time for taking a sickle to the corn, and gathering it in stooks in the field, ready to be pitch-forked up onto an ox-drawn cart and hauled off to the barns. It will eventually be threshed with flails, two lengths of wood joined by a chain, or by letting the oxen tread on it, so the grain is separated from the chaff, or husks.

Risking fines

Later all the grain is, or should be, taken to the lord's mill to be milled into flour – at a cost to the peasant. Through the year his wife takes bread dough to be baked in the lord's oven, for another fee. Some bold families use household querns to mill the flour, risking a court fine, then bake their own bread, risking another.

Autumn and winter

At the end of summer there are sheep to be sheared, fruit trees to be climbed and their fruit picked. The grapes will be trodden and the wine-making started. In October, after the fallow land is ploughed,

Haymaking – from a medieval calendar – a June activity.

the winter corn will be sown. The swine-herd will take the pigs to the woods to feed. Acorns will be gathered to feed the pigs.

November, sometimes early December, is the 'blood-month'. Many of the pigs, sheep and oxen are killed and salted to preserve them for winter meat. There are still tools to be repaired, blades to be sharpened, fences to be mended and ditches cleared.

But soon it will be Christmas again.

FEEDING THE FAMILY

The peasant family depends on the food it grows and that supply is always at risk. The peasant's father remembers a year when mice and hamsters destroyed most of a corn harvest, and other years when rain flooded the fields and there were very poor harvests. He recalls epidemics of diseases among the cattle and sheep.

Peasant produce

The family's food consists of vegetables and fruit from the croft garden, bread made from the corn harvest and meat from animals killed at the start of winter. The farmer himself does the slaughtering in the farmyard, sometimes with a neighbour to help. Most parts of the animal will be eaten, even the intestines. Brains and tripe are favourite bits.

Peasants picking fruit.

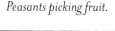

So once in a while there will be mutton, fatty pork, or beef, roasted or baked. People who live near the coast eat a lot of fish. The only other meat might be from animals the peasant has poached – a rabbit or a game-bird. But there are severe fines for infringing the lord's hunting rights. A fish or two from the stream is easier and less risky.

Daily fare

On most days, as well as bread, or instead of it, the family eats a kind of porridge or gruel made from oats and millet. Water or milk and

Daily diet

A 16th century German writer stated that:
❖ *...peasant food is poor quality bread, gruel, or boiled vegetables; whey is what they drink.* ❖
Other written and pictorial evidence suggests that the peasant diet was not quite so limited; but it was clearly not very varied, either.

Famine

A series of rainy summers and crop failures led to famine in several parts of Europe in 1438. A chronicler in Thuringia, Germany, recorded this:
❖ *In 1438 there was a huge rise in prices in Thuringia and elsewhere which led to a great famine, killing many people in their villages... Because people lay dead for a long time the air became polluted with a swiftly killing pestilence which caused the death of even more than had died of hunger.* ❖

salt are added to the grains of cereal, which is boiled for a few minutes. Flattened-out cakes of it can be fried to make a kind of crude loaf. The best bread, though, made from more expensive rye or wheat, usually needs yeast or sour dough to make it rise.

The garden plot

On the plot by the house the family grows vegetables, like turnips and cabbage. They have apple and pear trees and grow raspberries, strawberries and

A peasant couple slaughter a pig while others make bread.

blackcurrants. The hens give them eggs, the cows and sheep provide milk, butter and cheese.

Villagers drink water, whey, cider, and ale. The peasant doesn't trust the water and so drinks ale most often. He drinks mead occasionally, which is stronger, and is made from honey and water, boiled and left to ferment. His wife collects honey from her hives in the woods, where she also gathers wild herbs, dock and sorrel.

They may eat quite well some years, but hunger, and even famine, are part of the peasant's world. His father has told him about famine times, and seeing things eaten – horses for one – that he doesn't want to think about.

SICKNESS AND HEALTH

When the peasant's diet is poor, all kinds of illnesses visit the house. But even when food is plentiful, disease lies in wait, ready to strike, especially at the young. Funerals of babies and young children are a common sight in the village, and not just in times of pestilence. There is always the danger of babies and mothers dying in childbirth.

Pestilence

Deadly diseases strike every few years, it seems. There have been years of the 'sweating sickness', and regularly in the winter there are illnesses similar to it that have killed a number of people in the peasant's village.

Chesty coughs are common, and there is always the fear that someone in the family will get the type of consuming chest complaint that makes people sicken and die.

Other illnesses are more distant but still present threats. Sometimes lepers walk through the village with a bell. And there is madness: not only demons, but the planets and moon too, are believed to be able to cause it. It is believed that people born under the influence of Saturn are gloomy, and have skin complaints.

Many medicines were based on plants, just like today. Manuscripts called 'herbals' showed which plants could cure different diseases. Shown here are ivy (left) and a lime tree (right).

Medieval people believed that sickness was a punishment from God. In times of pestilence they took part in religious processions to try and appease what they saw as His anger.

Punishment for sin

Most illnesses though, or so the peasant believes, are God's punishment for sins. So he prays for good health for his family or for a cure when sickness strikes. He could even promise, some day when he has time, to go on a pilgrimage to a religious shrine.

For everyday troubles like toothache, colds and aches, the peasant's wife picks herbs as remedies; village women say they always work. You have to be careful though to collect herbs at the right time of day or night, when the right planet is in the right place for the cure. And you still need to pray to God as well.

Expensive doctors

Most peasants cannot afford doctors with their costly ointments, blood-letting and cupping. Town apothecaries are expensive with their compounds and medicines, like the 'treacle' well-off people buy, which comes from far away, takes 40 years to make, and is made of 100 ingredients including roasted vipers. That is the story the peasant hears, anyway.

People try charms and spells and chants too, which they think work sometimes. People who aren't doctors try blood-letting – sometimes with fatal results!

The Black Death

The Black Death of 1348 killed millions – a third of the population of Europe. A medieval doctor, Guy de Chauliac, wrote how the pneumonic, and then the bubonic, plague struck Avignon in France:

❖ *The plague began here in January and lasted seven months. There were two kinds. The first, with continuous fever and spitting of blood, lasted for two months; victims died within three days. The second, with continuous fever, and carbuncles and swellings, mainly in the armpits and the groin, lasted for the rest of the time, and victims died within five days.* ❖

WOMEN'S WORK

The peasant's wife makes bread and cooks for the family. She collects the firewood and makes the fire; she sweeps the house and does the beds. Then there are the children to be fed and clothed and looked after. She keeps a specially sharp eye on the baby and toddler, indoors and out. She washes and mends all the clothes; the underclothes are washed regularly, the outer garments much less often.

Dressmaker

The peasant's wife actually makes nearly all the family clothes too, some from the wool of their own sheep, which she has spun herself, and then woven into rough cloth, and some from the flax they grow which she has turned into linen. Some clothes she makes from lengths of cheap cloth she buys at the market, or at the door from travelling pedlars.

The family's clothes are grey or black, and have to last a long time, so they often look shabby. She and her family don't wear anything colourful, except on feast-days and holidays.

There are one or two rich peasants in the village who dress as if they think they are merchants, wearing coats with bright buttons and decorated belts, giving their wives long dresses and silk hoods more suited to living in the town.

Beekeeping produced honey the peasant woman could sell.

Dressing down

'Sumptuary laws' aimed to prevent lower-class people from imitating the appearance of their superiors. A 13th-century German writer says that peasants can wear:

❖ *...grey, homemade breeches, and blue ones for holidays, made of good milled loden [cheap] cloth. No better colour was permitted either husband or wife.* ❖

Medieval facts

Fashion for peasants changed in later medieval times. Men's loose tunics were replaced by short vests and buttoned waistcoats, and by breeches more like trousers; women wore wider collars and more figure-fitting dresses, pleated from the hips, than they'd previously worn. The Church expressed disapproval of changes which meant more of the body was on show.

This manuscript illustration shows women trapping rabbits. Whether they could do so legally would depend on what rights their lord claimed over wild game.

Farmworker

As if all that work around the house isn't enough, she helps her husband out in the fields sometimes, with ploughing or haymaking. When her husband is in the fields she sees to the pigs, and the grazing sheep, and of course the hens and the ducks. She milks their cows and makes butter and cheese. And she goes out herself into the woods, collecting fuel for the fire and herbs for cooking or medicine, and seeing to her beehives and collecting their honey. To cap it all, she has gleaning duties at harvest, and of course has to walk to the manor-house with the eggs, hens, ducks, butter and so on that are all owed as dues at different times during the year.

The ploughman's wife

This unforgettable picture of the peasant's wife and children at work with him in the fields comes from *Piers Plowman*, by William Langland, a 14th century English poet:

❖ *His wife walked beside him with a long stick in a short coat with a winnowing sheet wrapped round her to keep off the cold. She went barefoot on the ice so the blood flowed. At the end of the row there was a small bowl, and in it lay a small child covered in rags, and two two-year olds were on the other side... and they all cried the same cry till it was sad to hear.* ❖

Weaving cloth on a loom.

The peasant pays some of his fines and taxes to the lord or the king in cash. To do this the peasant and his wife need to earn some money. Some of this extra income comes from selling the surplus vegetables and fruit from the cottage garden, or some of the eggs or meat from livestock.

Extra income

The family doesn't need to eat all the eggs from the hens and ducks, or all the raspberries and loganberries, or all the bacon from the pigs. The peasant's wife takes whatever they can spare and makes a few pennies selling what she can in the nearby town. The town is growing, and there is an increasing demand there for fruit and vegetables, bacon and mutton, milk and cheese, honey – exactly the things she can provide.

Medieval facts

The ways in which village women earned cash for their families might be by means of activities that the local manor court disapproved of. Emma Powel, a peasant woman of Ramsey, appears in the court rolls on charges relating to brewing ale, baking bread, working as a butcher, and selling 'pudding' – probably homemade sausage. She was evidently successful in what she did; the charges stretch over a 50-year period.

A visit to a town such as this one gave peasants a chance to sell surplus produce.

When the children are older she plans to add to her income by brewing and selling ale, as several other women in the village do, fitting it in between other tasks. It will not be 'strong' ale, but the peasant's everyday drink, which they have from early morning onwards. She hopes to sell about 90 litres (20 gallons) a week to make a bit of extra income.

Cash jobs

There are opportunities for the peasant himself to earn cash too, and not just be paid in 'kind', meaning in eggs, or lambs, or wood, depending on what work he does and for whom. Since he now has oxen, and a cart, he can work as a carter when his other work is done. Carting is always needed, for all kinds of materials: dung, timber, stone, peat, animals and foodstuffs.

Some of what he carts will be things he picks or gathers himself and takes to the town, or the manor-house, to sell: rushes or sedge for thatching, wood for fuel, or for the wood-turner in the town. He can catch fish with a creel and do a small amount of hunting too, of birds especially. He takes his bow in the cart with him, and his son, as a helper.

GAMES AND ENTERTAINMENT

Peasant life isn't all work. There are games that children and adults play together. There is music-making and sport. Everyone looks forward to the next holy-day or feast-day, when work stops. Alongside attending church services, these festivals are times for celebration and entertainment, with plays, dancing, minstrels, cudgels, pig- and bear-baiting, tilting, wrestling, music and drinking. They are a great release from the drudgery of working life, but not an excuse to run wild.

Christmas

Christmas is the best time. No work can be done in the fields, and the lord treats his tenants to a feast at the manor-house with food and ale. The peasant and his friends contribute by helping to bring in the yule log, taking their own plates, mugs and tablecloths, and by bringing bundles of brushwood to make sure the meat is not served raw. At the height of the fun, the human Hobby Horse gallops in, trying a horse-like neigh, tossing a painted wooden head and swinging a horse-hair tail.

A few days later there are the Twelfth Night fires, with food and drink around twelve small fires in the fields, or indoors – if it is raining – with candles.

Easter

At Easter, the peasant and his wife go to church frequently and give each other 'pace eggs' which are hard-boiled eggs, painted decoratively. Some neighbours

15th-century Christmas fun in the Great Hall of a noble house.

Nutcrack Night

What we call Hallowe'en was also 'Nutcrack Night'. A couple who were about to be married put two walnuts or hazelnuts, one each, into the embers of a fire. The nuts either crackled and split, for the love to come, or burnt silently, for future indifference:

❖ *If he/she loves me, pop and fly.*
If he/she hates me, lie and die. ❖

Easter

When Eleanor of Aquitaine came to England to be queen to Henry II (c.1122-1204) and a courtier was listing for her the many customs of the 120-day Easter cycle, she impatiently interrupted him:

❖ *But what is particularly Easterly?*
His answer:
Morris dances, mystery plays, and pace egging. ❖

At a conference in Calais, France, in 1439 to discuss terms at the end of the Hundred Years War between France and England, several participants failed to turn up because they had been injured playing football.

When local rivers froze, peasants could skate. Late-medieval winters were much colder than those of today.

walk to the nearest town to visit the fair, and to watch the 'mystery' plays, religious dramas performed by the men and women of a particular trade group.

The subject of the mystery play matches the profession of the group of tradesmen – or guild – that is putting it on. The carpenters put on a play telling the story of Noah's Flood because it was members of that craft who built the Ark.

On 1 May, men and women go out into the woods to cut a branch and bring it back to the door of their house. The peasant helps to erect the maypole in the village, to dance around, and looks forward to learning who will be queen of the May this year.

Sports and games

During the year there are sports and games in plenty – from cock-fighting, cudgels and wrestling, to quieter sports like archery, dicing and board-games, and fishing.

There are plenty of occasions, or excuses, for drinking strong ale. Each of the main events of the farming year demands its celebratory 'ale' – like the 'scythe-ale', when the corn is cut. And of course every village wedding needs its 'bride-ale'. There are also tithe-ales, Midsummer-ales, lamb-ales, Whitsun-ales and bid-ales – all stronger than the daily ale.

Medieval games included football (right) and hoop-rolling.

One game that is sometimes played on these occasions is 'bringing home the bacon'. Couples claiming they have not quarrelled in the last year are questioned about their claim. The couple that cannot be trapped in a lie or inconsistency wins a side of bacon.

FREEDOM

Freedom at a price

This is an extract from an 11th century grant of freedom to a betrothed French serf living on the lands of l'Abbaye de St Trond; there are one or two conditions, though:

❖ *I, Frederick, by the grace of God, Duke of Lothier, have given to the altar of the holy confessor, Saint Trond, a female serf, Imma by name, betrothed to a certain Azelino of Stalen, at the request of Adelard the abbot, so that her freedom may bring liberty to my soul in the presence of God… But the condition of this transfer is that she and her posterity shall pay one denarius every year to the altar of the confessor… And on their death they shall pay 12 denarii… They shall live as free persons without calumny… I have caused this charter to be written for them and the names of suitable witnesses who were present to be added to it.* ❖

In the worst times, the peasant has had thoughts of trying to escape from his tied land, with its endless labour, its services and fines. He has heard that if you run away and live on the demesne lands of the king or in a chartered town for a year and a day, you're free — if you aren't caught, brought back and fined for running away. Other men have been lucky enough to marry free women; that in itself has freed them.

Buying freedom

Gaining freedom is easier for those with less land, cottars or smallholders with 4 or 5 acres. They seem to be able to gain their freedom by paying the lord a modest fine. Some with more land can too, but they have to pay more. Freedom might also be gained by undertaking an obligation, like promising to return to the village court every so often, or coming back to work at harvest.

Those who wish to enter the Church gain their freedom. One boy in the village went to the monastery recently to learn Latin and become a priest. The boy will become free although his father has had to pay the lord a fee granting permission for his son to enter the Church. Only one or two peasants want a religious life for their sons, though.

Having made his fortune, a free man returns to the manor to help with the harvest.

One reason for falling yields from farming in the 14th century may have been a change in climate leading to summers of storm and wet. That and the plagues may have driven many peasants from their villages. This inscription on the wall of Ashwell Church was perhaps carved by a villager as he left:

❖ *The first plague was in June 1300.*
[Lower down:]
The plague or pestilence of 1349.
[Then:]
1350: wretched, wild and driven to violence the people remaining become witness of a tempest. On St Maur's Day this year 1361 it thunders on the earth. ❖

Leaving for the town

The peasant also knows he could escape to the town and look for paid work. He already earns some extra money from his carting and from his wife's sale of produce and her ale-brewing. Between them, they might eventually earn enough to buy most of their food instead of producing it from their land.

Villagers come and go. Some villagers have left for good. One widow on her own, whose son had gone off to school in the town, paid the various fines, rents and money payments instead of work-days and finally bought her freedom for 30 shillings.

There were 30 or more houses in the village once. Now there are only 20 or so. There is less social life now too, with only two ale-brewers. The peasant labours on.

A 14th-century Italian town. Many peasants from the country went to towns and earned enough to buy their freedom.

LAST DAYS

The peasant is old and ill, worn out with ceaseless labour. In his late forties, he has outlived several of his friends, and survived outbreaks of disease in the village.

Inheritance and fines

His land and possessions will pass to his children, but his widow is entitled to a third of everything while she lives. There will be the lord's claims on his inheritance – the heriot of the best beast and the fine on the tenement, as well as the church's right to take the second-best beast. He worries that the lord might demand a higher entry fine to the tenancy from his son, or try to change the family's holding to a lease, lasting for only a set number of years.

Fear of death

He fears death; he has been taught to by the priest's sermons and the pictures in church of pits of 'fire and brimstone', of fiends with blazing eyes ready to pitch-fork their victims into 'the great flaming of fire which is ten times hotter that any fire in this world'.

Neighbours call round. In a small village everyone is aware of an approaching death. No doctor comes, though. Only richer people in towns can afford doctors.

A parish priest anoints a dying man with holy oil as he gives him the last rites.

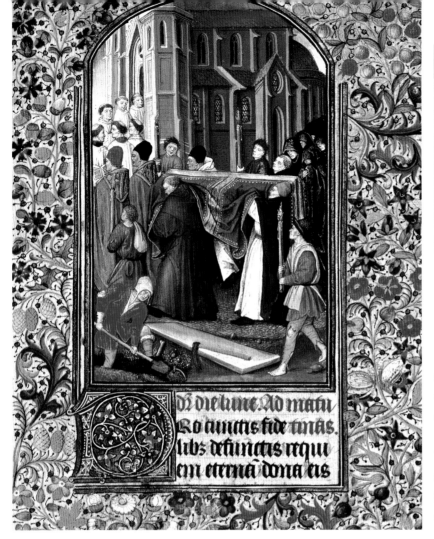

While the funeral takes place, a man digs the grave for the final resting place.

comes to administer the sacrament of Extreme Unction, the ceremony of the final anointing.

The peasant makes a final confession of his sins, and is given the bread and wine of the eucharist.

The priest

A small procession arrives at the home of the dying peasant, led by the priest who is followed by chaplains and clerks carrying a bell and a candle, holy water for sprinkling on the peasant, and oil for anointing him. With these the priest brings the power to grant absolution for the peasant's sins; he

Wake, and burial

When the peasant's short life is over, he is laid in the best room in the house. A fire is lit, candles burn, neighbours gather round.

Then comes the lychwake. Family, neighbours, friends and other farmers keep watch round the body through one long night. There will be cakes and ale.

They are all at the funeral, a few to carry the coffin from the church out into the yard. Most of the village crowds into the churchyard, where he is buried, on the southern, sunny side.

GLOSSARY

Acre ❖ a measurement – 2.471 acres = 10,000 metres square

Apothecary ❖ someone who mixes up medicines

Banns ❖ the priest 'calls the banns' three times in church, stating a couple's intention to marry and asking whether anyone has an objection to the marriage

Betrothal ❖ being engaged to marry

Bondman ❖ someone who is not free – a type of serf

Boon-days ❖ extra work days demanded by the lord of the manor

Cellarer ❖ a monastery official responsible for food supplies and trade with the world outside

Clerk ❖ a churchman, or a literate scholarly man, or someone looking after accounts

Commons ❖ grazing land and woodland within the village boundaries which could be used by all the villagers

Confession ❖ the private act of admitting sins to a priest

Cot ❖ a small house

Cottar ❖ a holder of a small tenement (5 acres average) with a small house

Court roll ❖ the record of a court's decisions, called a 'roll' because the parchment it was written on was rolled up

Cudgel ❖ a short stick used as a weapon and in sport

Demesne ❖ part of a manor farm directly farmed by its lord

Dowry ❖ a gift of money, land or possessions that a woman brought with her into a marriage

Due ❖ an amount to be paid

Fair ❖ lords were 'granted' fairs to allow the sale of goods of all kinds in one place, with stalls etc; entertainers and performers tended to arrive, too

Feudalism ❖ the system of holding land in return for agreed services or 'works'

Fine ❖ a fee or charge

Forest ❖ areas of woodland set aside specially for hunting

Free ❖ the condition of not being servile or 'bound' to the land

Furlong ❖ the length of a furrow, about 201 metres

Gleaning ❖ picking up ears of corn left on the ground by the reapers

Hamlet ❖ a settlement smaller than a village

Hand-fasting ❖ clasping of the hands in promising to marry

Hayward (or heyward) ❖ a village official responsible for arranging the hay harvest

Heriot ❖ a due payable to the lord on the death of a tenant, usually 'the best beast', sometimes the finest piece of clothing

Hide ❖ a measurement of about 120 acres (48 hectares)

Homage ❖ a vow of loyalty and allegiance to a superior

Lord ❖ the male tenant of a manor, usually a noble or knight; the 'lady of the manor' is a female with the same rights

Manor ❖ an area of land ruled by a lord, with its own manor court

Mark ❖ a coin worth 13 shillings and 4d (old pence) – about 65p

Mass ❖ the main religious service in the medieval Catholic Church, enacting the ceremonial consumption of bread and wine, 'the body and blood of Christ'

Money ❖ 1d (denarius)= 1p (one penny today), 240d = 100p, 20 shillings = £1, 1 mark = 13s 4d [65p]

Mortuary ❖ the due paid to the priest on a peasant's death, usually 'the second-best beast'

Mystery play ❖ a biblical story acted out by members of a craft guild

Nobles ❖ high-ranking people such as lords and archbishops; also a coin

Payment in kind ❖ payment with articles of produce, like eggs

Priest ❖ the clerk in charge of the church; sometimes a rector or vicar (meaning substitute for rector)

Plighting troth ❖ making a promise to marry

Reeve ❖ a manor official elected from amongst villagers; his duties were to organise the peasants' work for the manor and ensure collection of their dues

Seize ❖ possess [being 'disseized' of land is being deprived of it]

Serf ❖ a 'servile' or unfree person 'tied' or 'bound' to land they hold from a lord; a 'bondsman' or 'villein'

Shepherd ❖ a peasant put in charge of village sheep

Slave ❖ a person in the absolute ownership of another

Swine-herd ❖ a peasant put in charge of village pigs

Tenement ❖ an area of land with a house attached, rented from a landlord

Threshing ❖ separating the grain from the stalks and husks by hitting the harvested corn with a flail – a long, hinged stick

Tithe ❖ the annual payment due to the church or lord of one-tenth of the villein's produce

Toll ❖ the right to make strangers bringing goods to town pay an amount [a 'toll'] on what they brought

Vassal ❖ someone who held land from a lord in return for vows of homage and service

Villein ❖ a peasant tied to the land, who farmed strips of land

Wake ❖ the ceremony of 'watching', overnight, the dead person's body before burial

Yardland ❖ about 30 acres (12 hectares); sometimes a 'virgate'

Yardlander ❖ a holder of a yardland

Useful medieval history websites

www.fordham.edu/halsall/sbook.html

A website where you can read many original documents.

www.trytel.com

A website that provides historical information about cities and towns during the medieval period and much original source material through its Florilegium Urbanum.

www.oxfordshirepast.net

For local source material, visit this website.

www.the-orb.net

The website for the On-Line Reference Book for Medieval Studies.

www.mnsu.edu/emuseum/history/middleages/

A website where you can focus on life as a medieval peasant, knight, nun or merchant.

For more detail visit:
www.pitt.edu
www.history.ac.uk

TIMELINE

c.1000 over the next 200 years the European population grows enormously

c.1000 a heavier wheeled plough, which cuts deeper, replaces the lighter 'hook' plough across Europe – more use of horses in farming

1066 William of Normandy invades England – and is crowned King

1096 the first crusade begins

c.1100 over the next 200 years, there is a great expansion of peasant settlement in Europe

c.1100 gradual introduction of the 'three-field' agricultural system across much of northern Europe

1135–54 civil war in England

1146–1254 further crusades - 2nd to 7th

c.1190 first windmills in Europe

c.1200 some peasant houses are being built of stone in northern Europe

c.1200 German peasant houses begin to introduce a smokeless stove (stube) to heat their homes

c.1200 horses replace cattle to pull heavy loads in northern Europe

c.1200 money rents gradually replace labour services – growth of towns, trade and the money economy

1205 the River Thames freezes and can be crossed over the ice

1207 the Order of St Francis is formed in Italy

1208 King John quarrels with the Pope, who bans church services in England

1252 Henry III is given a polar bear, which swims in the River Thames with a muzzle and chain

1260 the cathedral is consecrated at Chartres in France

1265 Marco Polo travels to the Far East

c.1270 the oldest paper manufacturing in Christian Europe at Fabriano, Italy

1279 new silver coins created in England – the groat (4d), round farthing and halfpenny

1285 spectacles are made in northern Italy

c.1310 the mechanical clock is perfected

1317 heavy rains and ruined harvests cause famine across Europe

1323–28 peasant revolts in the Netherlands

1337 the outbreak of the Hundred Years War between England and France

1344 the first English gold coin, the noble, is worth 6s 8d

1348-49 the arrival of the bubonic plague, 'Black Death', in Europe

1361 plague breaks out again

1362 William Langland begins to write his poem, *Piers Plowman*

1369 harvests fail across Europe

1381 the Peasants' Revolt in England

1387 Chaucer begins his *Canterbury Tales*

1388 the first town sanitation act is passed in the English parliament

1437-38 ruined harvests, famine and plague occur in many parts of Europe

1438-40 heavy rains and ruined harvests in England

1430-70 economic crises hit England – many peasants are ruined

1470 an economic revival begins

INDEX

These are the lists of contents for each title in *Medieval Lives*:

Peasant
Introduction · First years · Peasant cottage · Childhood
The Church · Marriage · Land · Work-service for the manor · The manorial court
The working year · Feeding the family · Sickness and health · Women's work · Earning money
Games and entertainment · Freedom · Last days · Glossary · Timeline/Useful websites · Index

Merchant
Introduction · First days · House and home · Growing up · School · Becoming a merchant
Marriage · The wool trade · Travel and communication · War and piracy · Secrets of success
Branching out · Wealth and property · The merchant's wife · Good works · Health and diet
The end · Glossary · Timeline/Useful websites · Index

Knight
All about knights · A future knight is born · Time to leave home · Becoming a squire
A squire goes forth · Becoming a knight · Invitation to the castle · Joust! · Called to war
Battlefield tactics · Dressed to kill · Weapons · Siege warfare · Pilgrimage · Returning home
Knightly duties · Death of a knight · Glossary · Timeline/Useful websites · Index

Nun
Introduction · Birth · Childhood and education · To the nunnery – postulant
The nunnery itself · Taking the veil – novice · Daily life – the offices · The inner life
Daily routine · Enclosure · Cellaress and librarian · The world outside · Priests and nuns
Poverty and personal possessions · A visitation · Difficult times · Death · Glossary
Timeline/Useful websites · Index

Lady of the Manor
A medieval lady · A lady is born · Invitation to a wedding
At home with a lady · Wifely duties · Noble children · A year in the life
Clothes and hairstyles · A lady's hobbies · A lady's books · Time to eat · The lady falls ill
Women who work · The noblest ladies · A visit to a nunnery · The world outside
Widowhood · Glossary · Timeline/Useful websites · Index

Stonemason
Introduction · Birth · Childhood and growing up · Training - the quarry
Training - the building site · Rough-mason – a bridge · Summoned to work - a castle
A real 'mason' - the abbey · A growing reputation · Stone-carver · The lodge
Under-mason for the college · Master-mason for the cathedral · Designing the cathedral
Building the cathedral · Retirement · End of a life · Glossary · Timeline/Useful websites · Index